LEARN ICT

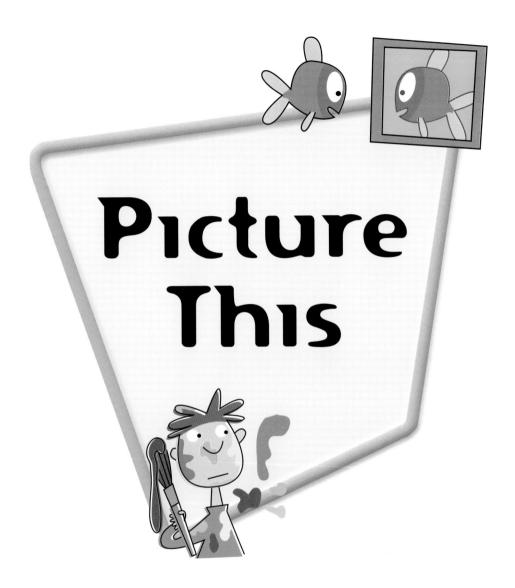

Picture This

Anne Rooney

QED Publishing

First published in the UK in 2004 by
QED Publishing
A division of Quarto Publishing plc
The Fitzpatrick Building
188–194 York Way, London N7 9QP

A Catalogue record for this book is available from
the British Library.

ISBN 1 84538 039 8

Written by Anne Rooney
Consultant Philip Stubbs
Designed by Jacqueline Palmer
Editor Anna Claybourne
Illustrator John Haslam
Photographer Ray Moller
Models supplied by Scallywags
Additional artwork by Luki Sumner-Rooney

Creative Director Louise Morley
Editorial Manager Jean Coppendale

Printed and bound in China

The words in **bold** are
explained in the Glossary
on page 31.

Contents

Imagine how boring all the things you read would be without pictures. Pictures liven up the page or screen, grab your interest and even help explain things.

Making pictures

In your own work, you can add pictures by drawing with pencils or pens, or by making pictures on the computer. You can even do a picture partly by hand and partly with the computer by scanning in a picture and then adding to it on screen.

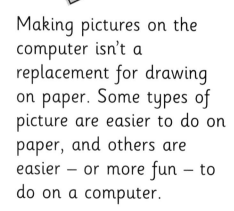

Making pictures on the computer isn't a replacement for drawing on paper. Some types of picture are easier to do on paper, and others are easier – or more fun – to do on a computer.

When do I need a computer?

The computer's great if you want to try out ideas, make a repeating pattern or draw a detailed plan. And if you want pictures to put in a web page or in a presentation you're making on screen, using the computer is the only way.

Pictures made using a computer are sometimes called 'computer graphics'.

This book is all about making pictures on the computer. You'll find out how to make all kinds of pictures, from paintings and drawings to plans, collages and even trick photos.

Think first

When you're making a picture on the computer, think first and plan what you're going to do.

Who, what, why, how?

Ask yourself these questions before you begin:

• What's my picture for?

The aim of your picture is called its **purpose**. For example, it could be to explain an idea, decorate something or illustrate a story.

• What should it be like?

Look at lots of pictures to help you decide what you like, and you'll soon learn how pictures work, what is most effective, and why. This is often called developing your 'eye'.

• Who's going to look at it?

The people who will look at your picture are called the **audience**. If you put up a poster, the audience is everyone who walks past. If your picture's in a newsletter, anyone who sees the newsletter is your audience.

• How are you going to use it?

Think about how your picture will be used. Is it a logo, an illustration for a story or a picture to put on a card? Plan the type, size and style of the picture to make sure it works.

Types of picture

You can make two very different types of picture on the computer – paintings and drawings. They work in different ways and you can do different things with them.

Paintings

In a painting, you fill in areas of the screen with different colours and patterns. You can find out about painting from page 8 onwards.

Drawings

In a drawing, you build up a picture using lines and shapes – sometimes called **objects** – that can be moved around. You can find out about drawing from page 14 onwards.

Have you seen Tigger?

Paintings

In a painting program, you make a picture by changing the colour of different areas of the screen.

How painting works

A computer screen is made up of tiny dots of colour, called **pixels**. The computer remembers a painting by keeping track of which colour each pixel has to be.

Colour palette

The colour palette gives you a choice of colours. Click on the colour you want to use – then use your mouse to paint with it.

With a painting program, you can go over any mistakes easily or repaint a whole area if you change your mind.

DO IT!

Open up your painting program and you'll see a blank painting area with a selection of tools and colours. Use your mouse to select the ones you want to use.

When you are using a computer, you don't need to decide on a colour in advance – you can try out lots of different colour schemes.

Toolbox

The tool set or toolbox lets you choose different ways of painting. To choose a tool, just click on it.

Painting tools

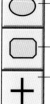

The pencil draws a really thin line.

An airbrush or aerosol can 'sprays' paint on the picture.

The flood fill tool fills large areas with colour.

The rubber is for rubbing out lines and shapes.

There are usually several brushes for painting lines of different thicknesses.

Other tools make simple shapes and straight lines.

Hold down the Shift key when using the rectangle or ellipse tool to get a square or circle.

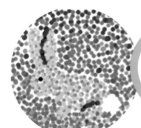

Make a **Pointillist** picture by adding spots of colour with a brush.

Background colours

When you start, your painting will probably have a white background. You can change it with the flood fill tool. It has a picture of paint pouring out of a pot.

When you've selected the flood fill tool, pick a colour and click on the background to fill the page with it. You can also use it to fill in shapes, and your program may also let you flood fill areas with patterns.

You can use shapes, lines and the flood fill tool to make a **Mondrian**-style painting.

All change!

It's much easier to make changes to your paintings on the computer than it is on paper.

Moving and copying

You can select (choose) an area of the picture and then move it around, make copies of it or just delete it.

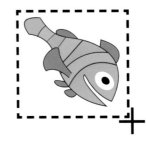

DO IT!

Click the 'select' tool and use the mouse to draw a rectangle over the part of the picture you want to select.

To remove part of the picture, choose 'Cut' or 'Delete' from the menus.

To copy it, choose 'Copy'. Choose 'Paste' to stick the copy you've made somewhere else.

To move an area of your picture, select it and drag it to where you want it.

Multiple copies

You can use 'Paste' to add lots of copies. Paste lots of copies to make a pattern.

More changes

Look for these options, too, and try them out:

- Rotate

- Flip

- Reflect or Mirror

Oops!

If you make a mistake and want to go back, look for an 'Undo' option. Save your painting with a different name every few minutes – then you can go back several stages if you change your mind.

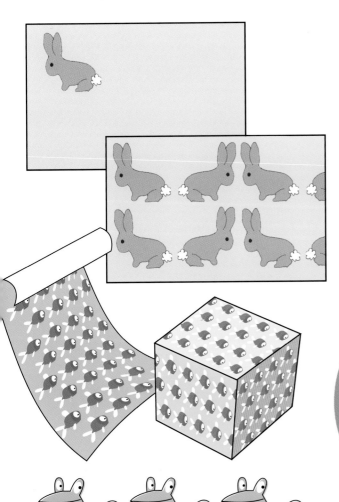

Working with photos

If you have a **digital camera**, you can use photos as the starting point of your painting. With a **scanner**, you can scan photos from paper into the computer to work on them.

Putting photos into your computer

A digital camera takes a photo and stores it on a computer chip instead of on film. You can copy it straight from the camera onto your computer and open it in your painting program.

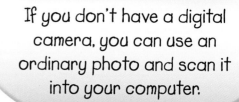

If you don't have a digital camera, you can use an ordinary photo and scan it into your computer.

 DO IT!
Open your photo using your painting program. Then you can add extra bits to it using the paintbrushes and other tools.

Cropping

You can crop a picture to cut it down to just the bit you want to use. You will probably need to select the bit you want to keep and then use a crop tool or option, but check how your program works.

Adding words

To add words to your picture, you have to use a text tool. This lets you type the words and pick the **font** (style) and size of letters you want. It usually appears in the toolbox as either the letter A or the letter T.

Love from Jack

Speech and thought bubbles

To add a speech or thought bubble to a photo (or other picture), first add a shape for the bubble, and then add text on top.

Drawings

When you use a drawing program to make pictures, the computer remembers your picture by keeping a record of where lines and shapes start and end.

When to draw

If you want to be able to draw accurately and maybe move parts of your picture around, a drawing is often better than a painting.

You need different types of computer programs to make paintings and drawings. However, some word-processors will let you make drawings. If you have a word-processing program, look for a 'Drawing' toolbar or menu option.

Objects

A drawing is made up of objects – things like lines and shapes. In a drawing, you can select a line or a box and move it somewhere else. (In a painting, a line or box is just a collection of coloured pixels, so all you can do is select the area it's in.)

In a painting, you can only move whole areas of your picture.

In a drawing, you can move each object by itself.

DO IT!

Look in your drawing program for a toolbox that will let you create different objects – such as boxes, circles, ellipses, straight lines and curved lines. Click on a tool to select it. It may stay selected or you might need to double-click to keep it selected.

Adding words

You can add words to your drawing, too. You can choose the style and colour, and treat them like any other object. This means you can reverse them, stretch them and move them.

Object styles

When you choose a drawing tool, you can often make extra choices – like how thick the lines should be, or whether a shape will be empty inside or filled with colour.

Reflection
Reflection

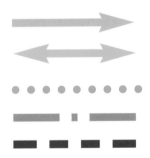

Lines can be given different styles, such as dotted or arrowheaded.

Shapes can be outlines, fills or filled outlines.

Because each object in a drawing is a separate thing, you can move or change one without changing any other parts of the picture.

DO IT!

To move or change an object, you first have to select it. Look for a tool that looks like an arrow.

Click on the arrow and then on the object you want to select.

Start making changes

Once you've selected an object you can:

• Move it – just put the mouse over it, hold down the mouse button and drag the object.

• Change the size and shape. Drag a corner handle to make it bigger or smaller while keeping it in proportion.

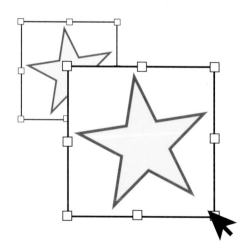

Get a handle on it

When you select an object, little blocks usually appear at the ends, corners or edges. These are called **handles**.

More changes

• Drag a handle on one side to distort an object, squashing or stretching it.

• Change the colour. If you select an object and then click on a new colour, the colour of the object will change.

Make a pattern

Copy an object and paste it in lots of times to make a repeating pattern.

Make a poster

You can decorate posters with drawings made up of simple shapes. If you need lots of similar things in your picture – like lots of hats – draw one, copy and paste it, and then make changes to the copies.

Jumble Sale

At Jedley School
Sat 10 May, 2-4pm

17

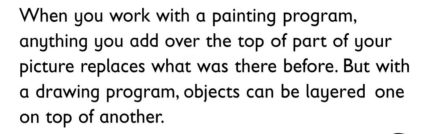

Pile it up

When you work with a painting program, anything you add over the top of part of your picture replaces what was there before. But with a drawing program, objects can be layered one on top of another.

Transparent sheets

Imagine a pile of transparent sheets — like the plastic sheets used for overhead projectors. This is how layering objects works. Each thing you add to the picture in a drawing program is like a new sheet laid on top.

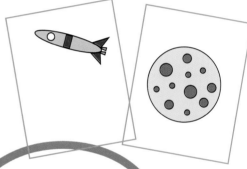

If you take one sheet away, the others stay the same.

If you put the sheets in a different order, different parts of the picture come to the front.

Order, order!

If your objects overlap or are layered, you might want to rearrange them to make a different pattern or picture, or so that you can see one that's hidden. To do this, you'll need to move the front object aside or send it further down the pile.

DO IT!

Click on the object in front and look for a menu option called 'Send to back' or 'Move back'. This will send that object to the bottom of the pile.

This object is at the front.

This object is at the back.

By arranging the objects in a different order, you can make a different pattern.

You might also need to reorder the objects if you want to select one that's at the bottom or middle of the pile.

Making plans

A plan is a drawing that helps you design or arrange something. For example, a **plan** of your bedroom would show where your bed is, where the door and window are, and so on.

To scale

The best plans are drawn 'to **scale**'. This means that the sizes of the things on your plan relate to their real sizes. For example, in a plan of a kitchen, if the table is twice as long as the freezer, then on the plan the table must be twice as long as the freezer too.

To draw a scale plan, you need to decide the scale – that is, the relationship between sizes in the real world and sizes on your plan.

A scale of 1:10 means things are ten times bigger in the real world than in your drawing. So if your kitchen was 2.5 metres long, you'd draw it 25 centimetres long on the plan.

Remember, you can add text to your drawings – so you can put labels and notes on your plans.

On the grid

Most drawing programs have a grid you can make objects 'snap' to. This helps you position objects accurately so that it looks neat.

In this picture, the corners of the box are snapping to the grid.

In this picture, the box is not snapped to the grid.

DO IT!

Look for a button or menu option called 'Grid' or 'View grid'. This will display a grid that will help you line up parts of your picture or plan. You should be able to choose whether objects snap to the grid, and you might be able to set the grid spacing.

Gran's garden

Our classroom

Lots of things

Plans often include several copies of the same object. For example, a plan of your classroom would have lots of desks and chairs in it, all the same size as each other. You only need to draw one of each – you can copy and paste to get all the others.

Make a model

You can use the computer for graphic modelling, too. This sounds really impressive, but it's not hard. A **model** lets you try out different ways of doing something without actually having to do it.

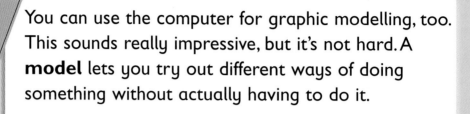

From plan to model

A plan of your room can be used for modelling. You can move the furniture around on your plan to try different arrangements for your room without actually having to shift heavy beds and wardrobes. When you've found an arrangement you like, you can then move the furniture.

If you were re-designing your room from scratch, you could try different sizes of furniture. Maybe you can get shelves in three lengths. Using a graphic model, you could try out all three sizes to see which will work best.

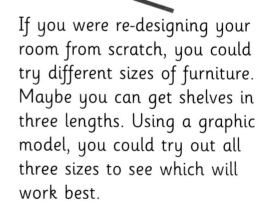

Designer dreams

Designers work with graphic models all the time. If a designer wants to make up a new car, a new outfit or packaging for a new product, they start with a drawing. If the drawing's on the computer, they can make lots of changes to try out different colours, shapes, sizes and styles.

Version 1

Wanda's fish food

keep your fish...

strong

and healthy

Version 1

Version 3

Version 2

Wanda's fish food

We're healthy

and strong

Version 2

Before you start experimenting, save a copy of your basic drawing or plan as a template. You can copy it and use it to make lots of designs, then choose the one you like best.

Perfect!

Few artists or illustrators get their work totally right first time. Checking and **reviewing** is an important stage in any piece of work.

Take a look

Check your picture on the screen before you print it out on paper. This lets you see if it's too big for the page, if you've missed anything out or if there are any mistakes.

DO IT!

Look for a 'Print Preview' option to see how your picture will look when it's printed.

You could ask someone else to take a look at your work and tell you what they think.

File formats

If you're going to use your picture in a web page, presentation or word-processed document, you'll need to save it as the right type of file. Check what you need for your final piece of work.

If you're making a web page, for example, you'll need to save your picture as a .GIF or .JPEG file.

If you're pasting it into a word-processed project, it can be a .BMP file.

Last-minute changes

Even if your picture looks brilliant, is it the best it can be? Maybe it could be improved. You should always review your work, and perhaps change it to make it better.

Finished!

When you've made any corrections or changes, save your work again before you print it out. Print one copy for a final check, before you print any extra copies you need.

Projects to try

It's time to try your computer graphics skills out for yourself. Here are some suggestions for projects but, of course, you can change them to make them fit in with your own interests.

Design a T-shirt

– and then make it, just like a real designer!

You'll need special paper that lets you transfer a picture onto a T-shirt. You have to iron the design on, so line up an adult to help you.

Doing the design

Start by drawing a T-shirt template and try out different designs. Save each design you like, then print them out and compare them. Pick the one you like best and review it to see if you can improve it.

When you're happy with your design, print it out once more on ordinary paper to check it will look right on your t-shirt before you use your special paper.

The finished shirt

To make your T-shirt, you'll have to print the design onto the special paper, then iron it from the paper onto a clean T-shirt. To make sure you get this part exactly right, you'll need to follow the instructions that come with your T-shirt transfer paper.

Remember, what will appear on your T-shirt will be a mirror image of your printout.

Planning a play area

Try using planning and modelling to redesign a playground or play area.

Draw a plan of part of your school, such as the playground, or maybe the home corner in the nursery classroom. Draw it to scale if you can.

Try moving the items in the plan around and adding new items that you think would make the area better or more fun. Save each version with a different name.

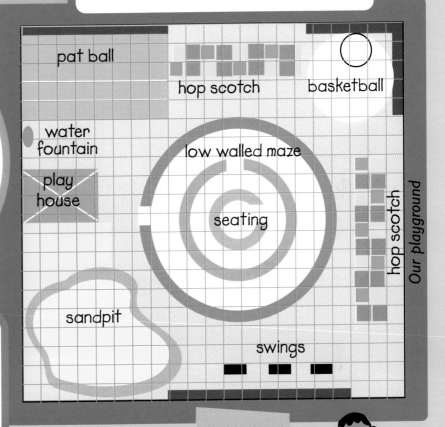

pat ball

hop scotch

basketball

water fountain

low walled maze

play house

seating

hop scotch

Our playground

sandpit

swings

Label your plans to show what each item is.

Print out and compare several of your plans. You could make a 3-D model of the best one using Lego or cardboard.

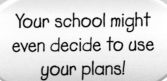

Your school might even decide to use your plans!

More projects to try

Make a collage

Use the computer to help you design patterns and draw pictures that you can use in a **collage** scene — maybe an underwater scene, a jungle scene or a busy town.

Print out your designs and pictures and cut them up. Collect and cut out other patterns and pictures you like from magazines, paper bags, advertising leaflets or anything else.

Put it together

To make your collage, arrange all the pictures and patterns you've collected on a large piece of paper. Try different arrangements of the pieces and glue them all down when you are happy with how the collage looks.

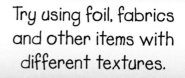

Try using foil, fabrics and other items with different textures.

Can you work out how to do a collage on the computer, copying parts from pictures and photos, and layering objects on top of each other?

Trick photo

Why not make a card for Christmas or another occasion from a photo?

If you use a digital or scanned photo, you can add shapes and text to it on the computer.

For example, you could use a photo of yourself or your pet and add cartoons or speech bubbles. Or you could use a photo of a friend and give them wings or monster ears.

When your picture is ready, print it out at the right size and check it. When you're sure it's right, print lots of copies.

For a party invitation, you could give the people party hats and decorate the photo with stars and spirals.

To make cards to send to your friends, stick each copy to the front of a piece of cardboard folded in half.

Grown-up zone

Picture This and the National Curriculum

This book will help a child to cover work units 4B, 5A and part of 6A of the IT Scheme of Work for the National Curriculum for England and Wales.

The National Curriculum for ICT stresses that ICT should be integrated with other areas of study. This means that a child's use of ICT should fit naturally into other areas of the curriculum. It can be achieved by tasks such as:

• Using a painting program to reproduce the techniques of painters such as Mondrian, Monet or Picasso.

• Using a drawing program to produce plans or maps to use in a geography or technology project.

• Making artwork on the computer to use for packaging designs for technology projects.

• Making artwork on the computer to include in word-processed reports.

• Making web pages or multimedia presentations on history or literature topics.

Children should incorporate planning, drafting, checking and reviewing their work in all projects. They should discuss with others how their work could be improved, whether ICT methods are the best choice for a given task and how ICT methods compare with manual methods. They should look at ways of combining ICT and manual methods of working.

National Curriculum resources online

ICT programme of study at Key Stage 2 in the National Curriculum:

www.nc.uk.net/nc/contents/ICT-2--POS.html

On teaching ICT in other subject areas:

www.ncaction.org.uk/subjects/ict/inother.htm

ICT schemes of work
(you can download a printable copy)

www.standards.dfes.gov.uk/schemes2/it/

The schemes of work for Key Stage 2 suggest ways that ICT can be taught in years 3–6.

Further resources

There are a lot of fun art resources on the web. Try:

www4.vc-net.ne.jp/~klivo/soft/mondrian.htm

Click on the canvas to generate random Mondrian-style paintings.

www.mrpicassohead.com

Make your own Picasso-style paintings.

http://snowflakes.lookandfeel.com/

Learn about symmetry with this virtual snowflake-cutting program.

Glossary

Audience

The people who you hope will look at your work.

Collage

Picture made up of pieces of other pictures and patterns, fabrics and even small objects.

Digital camera

Camera that stores pictures in a computer chip rather than on a film.

Font

Style of letters; all the letters in a font have a similar appearance.

Handle

Block on the side or corner of a selected part of a picture; you can move the handles to change the size and shape of that part.

Model

A copy of a real object or scene, used to try out how it would look or work.

Mondrian

Piet Mondrian (1872-1944), a painter who made pictures from blocks of colour and lines.

Object

Item in a drawing, like a shape or line, that can be moved on its own.

Pixel

Tiny dot on the computer screen.

Plan

Drawing that accurately represents something in the real world.

Pointillist

Type of painting made up of lots of tiny coloured dots.

Purpose

The aim of your picture.

Review

Look through and check.

Scale

Relationship between the size of an object in a drawing and in real life.

Scanner

Device for copying pictures from paper into the computer.

Index